You're Never Out of Style

Artwork by

SANDY LYNAM CLOUGH

HARVEST HOUSE PUBLISHERS
Eugene, Oregon

You're Never Out of Style

Text Copyright © 2000 Harvest House Publishers
Eugene, Oregon 97402

ISBN 0-7369-0387-9

Design and production by Garborg Design Works, Minneapolis, Minnesota

"There's something so stylish about you, Anne," said Diana, with unenvious admiration. "You hold your head with such an air."

LUCY MAUDE MONTGOMERY
Anne of Green Gables

Do you know how incredibly special you are? You are so lovable, a great friend, and absolutely unique. God has placed in your life certain gifts and abilities that shine. May these wise old sayings and encouraging Bible verses remind you of the courageous, cheerful, hopeful, beautiful, and loving person He is making you to be. Life is a journey, but no matter what stage you are at, you are never out of style.

Everyone has inside himself a piece of good news! The good news is that you really don't know how great you can be, how much you can love, what you can accomplish, and what your potential is!

ANNE FRANK

God never puts any
person in a space too
small to grow in.

AUTHOR UNKNOWN

"For I know the plans I have for you," declares the
Lord, "plans to prosper you and not to harm you,
plans to give you hope and a future."

THE BOOK OF JEREMIAH

*You are as welcome
as flowers in May.*

CHARLES MACKLIN

Let us be grateful to people
who make us happy; they are
the charming gardeners
who make our souls blossom.

MARCEL PROUST

6

There are persons so radiant, so genial, so kind, so pleasure-bearing, that you instinctively feel in their presence that they do you good, whose coming into a room is like the bringing of a lamp there.

HENRY WARD BEECHER

7

Cheerfulness keeps up a kind of daylight in the mind, and fills it with a steady and perpetual serenity.

JOSEPH ADDISON

My friends have made the story of my life. In a
thousand ways they have turned my limitations into
beautiful privileges, and enabled me to walk serene
and happy in the shadow cast by my deprivation.

HELEN KELLER

She had that indefinable beauty that comes from happiness, enthusiasm, success—a beauty that is nothing more or less than a harmony of temperament and circumstances.

GUSTAVE FLAUBERT

10

Excitement hung around Anne like a garment, shone in her eyes, kindled in every feature. She had come dancing up the lane, like a wind-blown sprite, through the mellow sunshine and lazy shadows of the August evening.

LUCY MAUDE MONTGOMERY
Anne of Green Gables

11

Your attitude about who you are and what you have is a very
little thing that makes a very big difference.

THEODORE ROOSEVELT

Every heart that has beat strongly
and cheerfully has left a hopeful
impulse behind it in the world, and
bettered the tradition of mankind.

ROBERT LOUIS STEVENSON

Enthusiasm is the best protection in any situation.
Wholeheartedness is contagious.

DAVID SEABURY

Duty makes us do things well, but
love makes us do them beautifully.

UNKNOWN

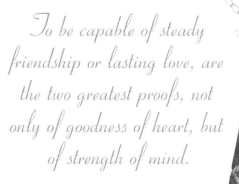

To be capable of steady friendship or lasting love, are the two greatest proofs, not only of goodness of heart, but of strength of mind.

WILLIAM HAZLITT

15

May happiness touch your life as warmly as
you have touched the lives of others.

AUTHOR UNKNOWN

*An inexhaustible good nature is one
of the most precious gifts of heaven,
spreading itself like oil over the troubled sea
of thought, and keeping the mind smooth and
equable in the roughest weather.*

WASHINGTON IRVING

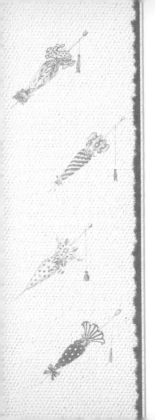

The person who
can bring the
spirit of laughter
into a room is
indeed blessed.

BENNETT CERF

Just being happy helps other souls along;
Their burdens may be heavy and they not strong;
And your own sky will lighten, if other skies you brighten,
By just being happy with a heart full of song.

RIPLEY D. SAUNDERS

19

Joy is a light that
fills you with hope
and faith and love.

ADELA ROGERS ST. JOHNS

You are today where your thoughts
have brought you; you will be tomorrow
where your thoughts take you.

JAMES ALLEN

Commit to the Lord
whatever you do, and
your plans will succeed.

THE BOOK OF PROVERBS

One loving heart
sets another on fire.

AUGUSTINE

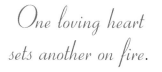

Nothing in this world is
impossible to a willing heart.

ABRAHAM LINCOLN

Friendship is a spiritual thing.
It is independent of matter or
space or time. That which I love in
my friend is not that which I see.
What influences me in my friend is
not his body, but his spirit.

JOHN DRUMMOND

Sweet souls around us watch us still,
Press nearer to our side;
Into our thoughts, into our prayers,
With gentle helping glide.

HARRIET BEECHER STOWE

When we're at low ebb, sometimes just to see the goodness radiating from another can be all we need in order to rediscover it in ourselves.

KATHLEEN NORRIS

There is divine purpose in bringing
out the best in one another.

DENIS WAITLEY

I thank God, my friend, for the blessing you are...for the joy of your laughter...the comfort of your prayers...the warmth of your smile.

AUTHOR UNKNOWN

28

Those who wish to
sing always find a song.

SWEDISH PROVERB

A cloudy day is no match
for a sunny disposition.

WILLIAM ARTHUR WARD

A willing heart adds
feather to the heel.

JOANNA BAILLIE

There is no personal charm
so great as the charm of a
cheerful temperament.

HENRY VAN DYKE

Cheerfulness. . . .promotes health and immortality. Cheerful people live longest here on earth, afterward in our hearts.

ANONYMOUS

He is greatest whose strength
carries up the most hearts by
the attraction of his own.

HENRY WARD BEECHER

Blessed is the influence of one true,
loving human soul on another.

GEORGE ELIOT

Most look up and admire the stars. A champion climbs a mountain and grabs one.

AUTHOR UNKNOWN

35

Keep your fears to
yourself, but share your
courage with others.

Robert Louis Stevenson

They may forget what you said,
but they will never forget how
you made them feel.

CARL W. BUECHNER

37

I am glad that in the springtime of life there were those who planted flowers of love in my heart.

ROBERT LOUIS STEVENSON

While I wait for tomorrow,
I'd like nothing better than
to spend now with you!

AUTHOR UNKNOWN

The simplest things—a gentle word, a smoothing touch—bring joy and peace like summer rain.

Most of the important things in the world have been accomplished by people who have kept on trying when there seemed to be no hope at all.

DALE CARNEGIE

Early as it was, he was at the station next morning to see
Jo off, and thanks to him, she began her solitary journey
with the pleasant memory of a familiar face smiling its
farewell, a bunch of violets to keep her company, and
best of all, the happy thought, "Well...I've made a friend
worth having and I'll try to keep him all my life."

LOUISA MAY ALCOTT
Little Women

Kind hearts are the garden,
kind thoughts are the root,
kind words are the blossoms,
kind deeds are the fruit.

AUTHOR UNKNOWN

43

If I could give you one gift, my
friend, I'd give you the gift to see
yourself as others see you, so you
could see how special you really are.

AUTHOR UNKNOWN

He who has begun a good work in you will complete it until the day of Jesus Christ.

THE BOOK OF PHILIPPIANS

To know someone here or there
with whom you can feel there is
understanding in spite of distances
or thoughts expressed—that
can make life a garden.

GOETHE

Special people are those who allow
themselves the pleasure of being close to
others and caring about their happiness.

AUTHOR UNKNOWN

The very society of joy redoubles it, so that, while it lights
upon my friend, it rebounds upon myself, and the brighter
his candle burns, the more easily will it light mine.

ROBERT SOUTH

Which can say more than
this rich praise—that
you alone are you?

WILLIAM SHAKESPEARE

The comfortable and comforting people are those who look upon the bright side of life; gathering its roses and sunshine and making the most that happens seem the best.

DOROTHY DIX

The man who radiates good cheer, who
makes life happier wherever he meets it, is
always a man of vision and faith.

ELLA WILCOX

51

Exuberance is Beauty.

WILLIAM BLAKE

All gardeners live in beautiful places because they make them so.

JOSEPH JOUBERT

The timid and fearful first failures dismay,
But the stout heart stays trying by night and by day.
He values his failures as lessons that teach
The one way to get to the goal he would reach.

EDGAR A. GUEST

May he give you the
desire of your heart and make
all your plans succeed.

THE BOOK OF PSALMS

The work an unknown good man has done is like a vein of water
flowing hidden underground, secretly making the ground green.

THOMAS CARLYLE

If you begin the day with love in your heart,
peace in your nerves, and truth in your
mind, you not only benefit by their presence
but also bring them to others.

AUTHOR UNKNOWN

The beauty of the soul shines out when a man bears with composure one heavy mischance after another, not because he does not feel them, but because he is a man of high and heroic temper.

ARISTOTLE

Many a friendship—
long, loyal, and
self-sacrificing—rested
at first upon no
thicker a foundation
than a kind word.

FREDERICK W. FABER

The beauty of a woman is not in the clothes she wears,

The figure that she carries, or the way she combs her hair.

The beauty of a woman must be seen from in her eyes,

Because that is the doorway to her heart, the place where love resides.

The beauty of a woman is not in a facial mole,

But true beauty in a woman is reflected in her soul.

It is the caring that she lovingly gives, the passion that she knows,

And the beauty of a woman with passing years only grows!

AUDREY HEPBURN

A smile is a light in the window of your face that shows that your heart is at home.

AUTHOR UNKNOWN

How far that little candle throws his beams! So shines a good deed in a weary world.

WILLIAM SHAKESPEARE

There never was any heart
truly great and generous,
that was not also tender
and compassionate.

We have seen and known some people who seem to have found this deep center of living where the fretful calls of life are integrated, where *No* as well as *Yes* can be said with confidence.

THOMAS KELLY

Then it was that Jo...learned to see the beauty and the sweetness of Beth's nature, to feel how deep and tender a place she filled in all hearts, and to acknowledge the worth of Beth's unselfish ambition to live for others, and make home happy by that exercise of those simple virtues which all may possess, and which all should love and value more than talent, wealth, or beauty.

LOUISA MAY ALCOTT
Little Women

63

You are . . .

blessed of the Lord.	*led by mercy.*
THE BOOK OF GENESIS	THE BOOK OF EXODUS
kept in perfect peace.	*promised rest.*
THE BOOK OF PSALMS	THE BOOK OF MATTHEW
wonderfully created.	*so loved.*
THE BOOK OF PSALMS	THE BOOK OF JOHN